Licking the bed clean

Coypright © the authors

First published 1978
This edition published 2019

Teeth Imprints
34 Rosamund Rd
Oxford
OX2 8NU
U.K.

teeth.imprints@gmail.com

ISBN 978-1-5272-3519-9

Cover drawings by Stef Pixner

Introduction

Forty years later, it's a shock to remember that there was a time before branding, marketing, and the rampant individualism of the Facebook era. I'd almost forgotten the struggles we had, back then, to find our voices as women and as writers, not to mention why we published the book as a group, wrote the introduction as a group, aired our debates and disagreements with the kind of democratic good faith that nowadays looks like dazzling naivety.

Yet there is as little polemic in the poems themselves as there is prettiness or politeness. Rather there's imaginative energy, the search for authentic form, and the starkness which comes from necessity. The drawings, too, have the intimacy of a peek into the seraglio, only these naked ladies aren't posing, but pushing shopping-trollies, dancing, reading, tearing out their hair.

We knew that we were breaking new ground: unlike most publishers at the time, we knew there was a readership out there, and of course we were right. We had to reprint, and reprint again. It took the publishing world a while to catch up.

Reading the book now, I'm amazed by our honesty and openness. The risks we took back then – of being ignored or attacked or laughed at – make the hairs rise on the back of my neck. (Unbelievable to recall that this was a time when the brand new word 'sexism' raised hoots of derision.) I'm amazed by the confidence of these young women, and very proud of them.

Alison Fell, 2019

Original 1978 introduction

The five of us have been meeting for a year to produce this pamphlet and to support and criticise each other in our ongoing work, prose as well as poetry. We were nervous of showing each other our work, but the group helped us to develop and become proud of our writing and to develop confidence in our identity as writers. The poems were written and selected by each individual writer, then discussed and criticised in the group. This feedback sometimes influenced individual choices, but as a group we didn't assume the power to change or reject poems.

Lack of confidence runs deep in us, and underlay many of our discussions.
—*I think of it as my 'three timidities'. First, and most basic: is my experience important enough to write about? Second: is it important or 'right on' in relation to the Women's Movement? Thirdly: is it 'art'?*

'The right to write . . .'
—*Will anyone else understand or identify with my perceptions, or am I a freak? Is my own experience worthy, worth writing about?*
—*For me, it's: do I have the right to take up that much space?*

—My worry is: is my experience valid? Is it real?
We don't think this is just our problem. Cora Kaplan, after a study[*] of relatively well known English and American women poets from the 17thC to the 20thC, concluded that '... a very high proportion of women's poems are about the right to speak and write'.

Female subject-matter has generally been ignored or trivialised within the predominantly male literary tradition. Poetry in particular is often considered to be about 'eternals'; it's the form in which 'universal' human experience is distilled. But it has largely excluded the specific experience of women, of working class or black writers; more so than novels which don't aspire to the same 'universalism'. It's not only a question of subject-matter: '... the language most emphatically denied to women is the most concentrated form of symbolic language – poetry.'[†]

'I'm not sure if this is a feminist poem . . .'

... some of us muttered nervously before reading out to the group. We are all feminists of various kinds, but the selves revealed in our writing don't always match up to our ideals of what it is to be a 'true feminist'. We are a complicated mixture of what we were and what we're struggling to become. We aren't all agreed on what 'feminist poetry' is or should be, either as regards form or content.

'Where are you in the poem?'

One view emphasised starting from the 'I', the writer's own personal voice, as in feminist politics more generally; 'the war starts here.'

—Where are you in this poem? There's not enough of a personal voice in it for me; how were you feeling during the encounter? And it shows the woman only as a victim; it ignores her power and her anger. There's a merging of the writer's voice and the voice of the woman in the poem. I want to know which is which.

—I don't think we can or should try to pin down a particular form or subject-matter. We need to write about everything that matters to us, using all the voices we can to do it in; about things specific to our experience as women, and things that concern men too, but which we experience from our position as women. The 'I' can't do everything. In

---

[*] Cora Kaplan *Salt and bitter and good*, Paddington Press, 1975

[†] Cora Kaplan 'Language and gender' in Women's Publishing Collective *Papers on patriarchy* conference 1976, 30 Talbot Terrace, Lewes, Sussex.

that poem, the poet doesn't need to describe how she's feeling – it leaves the reader to feel it more strongly. It's powerful just because it's left unsaid.
—It's a scary way of writing because people can read it in different ways; I want to be in control of it all.
—But you were crying at the end of the poem. . . .
—Yes. Maybe all I'm saying is: it was too powerful for me.

'I'm lying in bed and I can't get up.'

Some of the poems brought to the group didn't clearly contain an awareness of feminist struggle and change. In some of them it wasn't obvious that the writers were feminists, or even women. Some of them were just saying: 'here is a city street', 'I'm lying in bed and I can't get up', 'I'm crawling across the park feeling awful, rejected. . . .' Our final selection included both the poems with most relevance to us as women, and those we like best as poems. Some directly raise issues of personal and wider political struggle, others show the influence of surrealism and zen. Some are funny, others sombre or angry or painful.

The women we 'ought' to be

We agreed that it's vital as feminists and writers to express what we are, even if it isn't what we would like to be, and to try and honestly grasp the tension of that contradiction.
—Otherwise we could end up presenting idealised pictures of the women we 'ought' to be. Then between those pictures and the idealised pictures of women we're presented with in the media, where will we be able to recognise ourselves in what we read?
—I don't think you should use the word 'idealised' for both, as if there's no difference between them. 'False stereotypes' describes the media images better.
—I used the same word because I think they both present a stereotyped picture of what 'ideal' women should be, though their content and sources are totally different. One is dominant and enshrines patriarchal values; the other has been developed in opposition to it and is in danger of promoting merely a reversed stereotype.
—I still disagree. I don't think they're the same. We need our own strong images to counter the ones we meet every day and grew up with. But I do think there's a danger of censoring ourselves, of developing 'orthodoxies' as to how we should represent ourselves and other women; it's very complicated. . . .

Is it 'Art'?
—What about standards?
—Standards are irrelevant to us, a bogey.... We should be suspicious of the elitism implied in them.
—But we already have standards; we revise our own poems, we criticise each other's work, we think we might not be 'good' enough ... it's liberalism to pretend we don't. Standards are about how well we get our experience across. About finding language that's appropriate, alive.... We owe it to ourselves and whoever reads the poems to write as well as we can, and to develop and assert our own standards.

Finally...
We hope this book will inspire other women to write and to publish. We produced it ourselves and will be happy to pass on what we have learned about funding and the mechanics of publishing.

CONTENTS

Alison Fell   13
   Butterfingers   14
   The Victors   15
   For Myself   17
   Atlanta Streets   18
   Maria Burke   20
   Girls' Gifts   23
   Love Song   24
   Blessed be your heart, Cursed be your name   25
   There is a disturbance   26
   For Ivan   27
   Saturday Night Fever   28
   Heritage   29
   Meeting   30

Stef Pixner   31
   high heeled sneakers   32
   Mighty Boot   33
   snake   34
   scarecrow   34
   I, Gustav Spielenblatt   35
   skull cap   35
   on the opposite side of the white stagecoach   36
   in the morning he glares at me   36
   the pain that i find in dust and disorder   37
   Joie de Lire   38
   the weeds the witch & the roses   40
   someone simple   41
   absence   42
   In the park gutted trees   43

You down there, in your bed down there	44
that world through the window is a barefaced lie	45
a poem from Wales	46

Tina Reid   47

Jill the Gripper	48
Morning on the Campsies	49
My boyfriend's Mum	50
Anniversary Invitation	51
Ann's Poem	52
My heart is alive	53
Tower Hamlets Cemetery	54
See you	55
Sleeper	56
He keeps	57

Michele Roberts   59

Women's entry into culture	60
Coniston New Year's Eve	61
therapy 1	63
therapy 2	64
I have been waiting to mourn	65
memories of trees	67
Go away; for P.	69
punkrock; and Cocksparrow sings	72
I am abroad in a strange land	74
the eldest son goes home	76
I have just come from the war	78

Ann Oosthuizen   81

Bulletins from the front line	82
I do not remember you with pleasure	84

Drawings by

Alison Fell 5, 11, 14, 17, 19, 24, 28, 30, 51, 58, 64, 66, 69, 77, 83, 85
Stefanie Pixner 33, 35, 39, 40, 43, 45, 48, 50, 52, 54, 73, 75, 79, 86

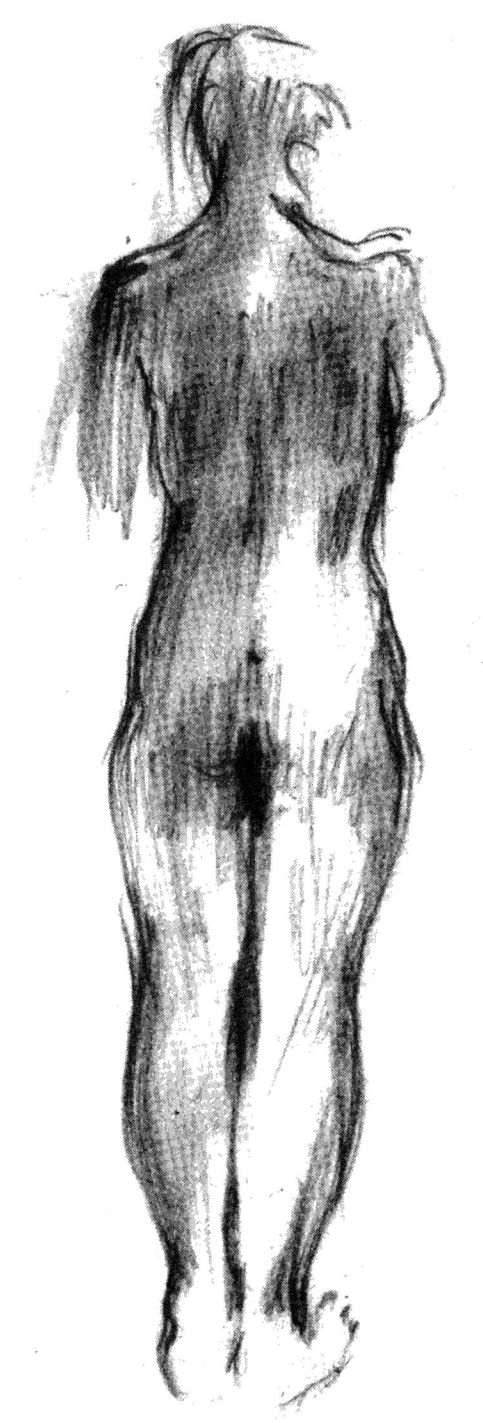

ALISON FELL

Butterfingers

At last I have heard
that yell my mother
staunched, for there she was,
a presence of a kind,
apronned, broad back
baking grudges;
she stuck it out, me
the mouse at her heel,
the trailing tail, skinny
squeak which wavered through
decades now thunders up

Mother you filled my mouth with flour
lover you splashed your white
in the bowl of me
these hands slippery from not
holding have let me crash,
such noise and crackle
such mess to mop

But at the yolk I run
yellow,
yellow and good.

THE VICTORS
October 18, 1977

What greater glory
than this
morning over
Bonn
with the sun
all in order
on the ranked
walnut trees
over
Mogadishu
and the three
slight shadows
on the airstrip
Dead
three more rebels
blood and sand
in their gullets
Dumb
three more silences
for the State

What greater glory
than this
morning over
Stammheim
with the sun
ekeing down
through gutters
slits
bars
blockhouses.

The chalkdust
hangs in sunbeams
marks time
marks place
marks corpses

gone
three more rebels
Baader shot
Ensslin hanged
Raspe shot

And Schmidt
by the ugly glint
of black cars
smiles to the
whirl of newsreel
how he rode
the night and won;
by drinking Coca-Cola
smoking sigaretten
taking snuff
made in Austria
by British mixers.
Callaghan simpers,
twinkles back victory
'A wonderful morning
for us all'

Six more silences
for the State,
the wrong voices
stilled
and the grey-faced liars
whirr out murder
till the roar
of right
deafens
us.

For Myself

In her
thirty-three year old
long grown
prime,
still the gnarled
changeling
peeks from her
cot,
ugly as a turnip
sheep-gnawed,
little sprout
which grew
in the dark
lives hardy through
frost,
etched
with a breadknife,
lonely as
black Hallowe'en,
fire hungers
in her lantern
eyes

Atlanta Streets

The timidest man owns streets
with his eyes – headlights sweeping
breasts, lips, thighs –
they dip only for a bigger bruiser.

Our lowered eyelids hide murder.

Outside a drugstore in Atlanta
one thug tried it on, for him
we waited, four of us fringing
the sidewalk, gangsters in the
shadows. One flung a chocolate malted
in his face, he lunged
kicked her down while we paused
(everyone hesitates who fears the murder
in her) but only for the time the bright
sour pink of a police car beacon
takes to spin once,
and then these sisters beat and clawed him
down and when he tried to run
I caught his coat-tails
and he spun back, roaring,
in an arc
into their fists again
and still I stalled there
until his buddy came to even up
the odds, then I was ready, but then
there was glass shattering
and the ruby razor neck of a
Coke bottle crooked up, glistening
and obscene,
and wise blacks hanging back
and white folks coming close – to
gawp? defend? who? us? him?
the staggering ravaged guy?

And now it was time to run, vault,
dodge trash, make
scant wind in the
still city dark, to the
car-park, rev through the underpass
shudder out to the
Freeway's tungsten howl

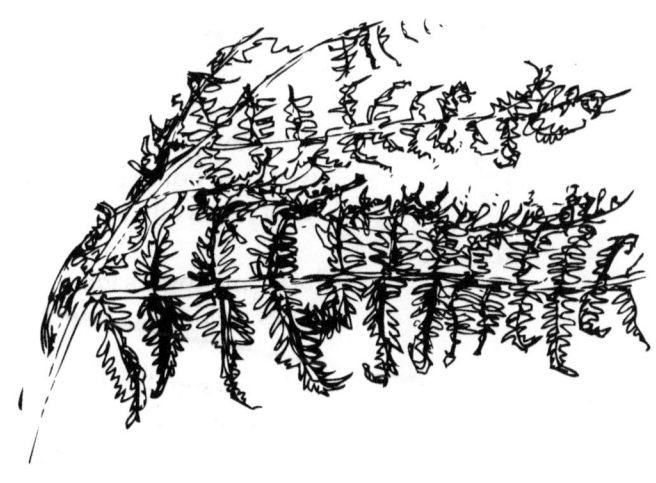

FOR MARIA BURKE
*(who knocked at the door while I was writing
  about the alienation of life in the cities under
  capitalism.)*

Maria, in search of hospitality:
I opened the door a crack
she stood there in the dark
dribbling a bit.
'We're in need of somewhere to stay'
She was alone. It was winter.
She wore plimsolls, her bare legs
were hairless.
'I used to know some man who lived here.
It's a squat, isn't it.'
'No, not a squat,' I snapped,
'And who was the man?'

The powerful deeply suspect
the powerless
of manipulations and lying.

'You should come in from the cold.'
Maria's eyes were fixed,
glassy on largactyl.
I phoned some hostels;
she knew them all and
loathed them, said she'd crouch
by frozen trees in the park
rather than go there.
'I went to a house I used to
live in, it was all pulled down'.

Clocks and towers loom over her
Homes shudder and tumble around her.

Her hands shook eating soup.
She accepted tea.
'It's the drug makes me shake'.
She'd hitched from a mental home

in Manchester, heading for another
in Southall, which didn't want her.
'I've a letter from the consultant.
Will you phone for me, tell him
I'm coming in?'
It was dated last June,
it said merely 'Dear Maria,
it was pleasant to see you
at the hospital today. What
I explained to you is that the drug
is a chemical which acts
on the brain and is necessary
to stabilise the thought processes.'

'It's my only home' said
the orphan angrily, 'I know
they don't want me but
I'm going in. I was there . . .
I lived there . . . three years.'
I showed her the spare room
she thanked me several times
stripped to her bra while
I was still there.
Only those with homes are entitled
to modesty, the consultant
is modest, his wife is modest
her body belongs to him only;
Maria's belongs to anyone:
the mouth to nurses who feed it
the head to doctors who shock it
the nipple to drivers on the open road
who pluck it
the smooth skin to the casual helper.

The consultant, who has all he needs,
considers her promiscuous, recoils
from the glare of her love that
stares from her eyes, seeking.

He reaches for a prescription pad;
this winter, he decides,
Maria must stand on
her own two plimsolls.

Maria gathering up
selves scattered like
grit on the roadside
doodles darkness
and a cottage with lit windows,
gropes and pines for her
three-minute-a-fortnight
father.

Girl's gifts

The soft whorls of my fingertips
against snapdragons:
I am making a flower basket for my grandmother.
A rose petal folds back, squares, curls under
One, two, many rose petals curl back
between my fingers
I search for the core which hides.
My grandmother is gentle today,
old. Bees hum over her.
Today she sits reading, not gardening,
not scolding.
The blossom on its branch holds juice which
a touch spills
I glance across the grass,
a shadow in the window is my mother
cooking, watching.
I am making a tiny secret basket for my grandmother.
My mouth waters
I would lick the green leaf, taste the bronze
and yellow silk of my snapdragon,
I mould petals, weave stems, with love
my little finger inches in the folds:
it is done, red and gold.
I will carry it cupped like a jewel or a robin's egg
It will lie, perfect, in her wrinkled palm
I will cross the grass and give it.

Love Song – the beginning of the end of the affair

I lie across your bed, love
Three cats and your children enfold me.
These necklaces I would never wear
for I was a wild boy-girl
at last
you, love
have twined them all around me.

Hungers move my heart now
but where will we touch, which
layers meet, my lovely flyer,
bird of air? You race, you soar,
raise winds, string perfect cloudstreams
in your wake.

But I am the woman with
one foot on the mountain,
my tread turns earth
and my stumblings are moving me beyond you.

Pinned to my mirror for you
I leave my blonde hair,
my pout, and other scraps,
refractions:
was that not all you wanted?

Rage I have now,
squalls of delight;
grief bursts hot and salt
on my cheek.
It's so lonely here
I wanted a companion.
But to ask you
is to see only your flinch,
and then a sudden shadow
in the corner of my eye
a mote in the sky
darting.

**'Blessed be your heart
Cursed be your name'**
(Howlin' Wolf)

Black voice high scarring
in the scrape of wood
drums, pulsed
base hollowed.
There was this moment
when one unashamed man
cried molten
powerless! needy!

before the grating
soul was strip-lit
piped out.
classless as supermarkets
top-rating
special offer

all's right with the white man
his songs roll down
smooth alleys
his dolls on the shelves
crisp as cornflakes
wait only for his munch

There is a disturbance

there is a disturbance:
stirrings through
the menagerie
raise the feathers
of the cock
and sleek the lion
with alarm

where is the man I
was prettying and prinking for?

*the streets foam
with white cars*

*sun rises, sets, rises
my teeth rend linen*

*storms straddle
earth and sky*

crawl of silence
in which leaves drip
and the devastation of
cities and circuses
is recorded

and with a new howl
a woman catapults
born. bloody. ready.

For Ivan, aged 9

He
is a small battlefield of loyalties
sturdy
still the night lies heavy on his chest
beasties bang on his doors
he fears his heart may stop

He
blushes when I sing sweetly
hurls his barrel self at my
arms open wide then draws back
remembering

Already he
yearns for past idylls
mother and father united
two beloveds in a double bed
under a single roof

He
passes hours
rosy-faced over flashing
river-fish, kicks his
feet like a crazy lamb and
sings up at the spring sun

He
tools precision pictures spiked
with armaments, thrills to
the sharp technologies of war

I fear for you unreasonably
I fear the day these wars or
others dry your wells and
lay you waste.
You who already have strength
to comfort,
bathe me in your laughter—
o moon face of innocence

Saturday Night Fever

Tonight I am all and always
dancer, a streak of a girl
shearing stars,
I'll kick a few out of
orbit
now I can make my real clatter
Mercury's grand to jive with,
and tap-dancing,
there's a thing!
— watch my bright rocket-feet.
I'll slew like fountains,
a feast of fireworks
each joint cradles quicksilver
each bone a hot song

Tomorrow limps
there's a stone in my shoe
no, a rock, jesus, a slagheap
Years of lead
Years of dread

Heritage

Grandmother I say to you
the red of the rowan
brings no ill-fortune

— Awa wi' ye!

Grandmother I tell you
I scorned the rule,
filed with your coffin
full way to the grave
and all your countrymen
stood stern, black hats
in their hands

— Awa wi' ye!

Warm May and
their hands on the rims
work-scourged
December raw

Aye, aye

Tall grass and harebells
swayed by the mound
and a whin-bush bent
yellow to the wind
but grandmother I tell you
the wired wreaths were
choked with laurel

— Awa wi' ye!

And where were the women?
And who stole the weeping?

Meeting

I am full up
with the worth
of the day's work
done
and rain-sleeked
I am
coming to you
through the crazy
tilt of umbrellas
and all their
avalanches
laughing like a wildcat

STEF PIXNER

high heeled sneakers

i dreamed Simone de Beauvoir and i
were climbing a mountain eating crepes
and wearing espadrilles. she carried
her alarm clock on her head
whereas i pulled behind me three train
carriages full of the things i thought
i might need for the journey.
we talked pleasantly of this and that. i
was trying to impress her with how
interesting i was coming from the post
war generation from a communist family
and being a woman but i had to stop
every now and again to change my
espadrilles for ballet shoes or army boots
or pick my nose or adjust a comma
on my hat or look at the view
or a word in the dictionary so that
she got to the top of the mountain before
me despite her years and
ate more crepes in the meanwhile
sitting on her alarm clock and waiting
for me and my train. when i got
there at last she said there are some
questions i've been meaning
to ask a woman of your
generation and so she began asking me
questions and i changed from my
army boots to a pair of high heeled
sneakers and back to espadrilles and then
back into ballet shoes. i've been meaning
to write you a long letter i said but just
then we saw a horde of mountain bears make
off with the luggage i'd so carefully
chosen and she still had a few books
to eat that morning so we exchanged
espadrilles and chinese postcards and
waved our red handkerchiefs
just as the lights went up.

Mighty Boot

He stroked her rest with lies.

'I am forging a mighty boot'
he said
'that we might dwell therein and
live content
I build this boot for you my dear
a token to our love.'
She smiled the smile of the simple soul
'I am forging a mighty babe'
she said
'that he might dwell within this boot
a token to our love.'

They smiled the smiles of simple souls
forged mighty boot and mighty babe
as tokens to their love —
then laced themselves inside the boot
and died for lack of air.

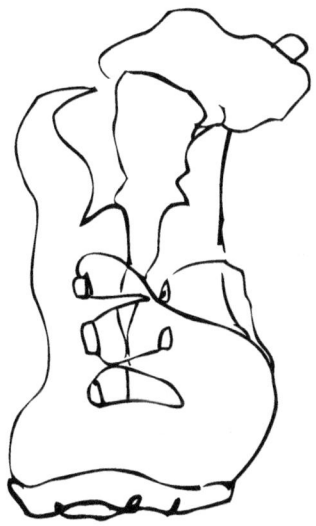

snake

along the cold street
a snake is marching
without boots
in silent slime
whistling a reptilian
melody in moving
scales.

it's night and only i
can hear its song and see it
slithering
with my shut eyes

noone is about
except this snake and me

and i'm sneezing.

scarecrow

the scarecrow
looks sad tonight all covered in rags
her solitude made of sticks
flapping in the dark field
and her eyes that won't shut
watching the cows at sleep.
with no shoes
and wind in her pockets,
she counts those stars
she can see
from her fixed angle
and listens to the black sticks rubbing
as she spits her curses at the moon.

I, Gustav Spielenblatt

I, Gustav Spielenblatt
walking down the corridors of lust
meet the ghosts of my forefathers,
their cocks covered in dust

skull cap

skull cap
draw the latch

if the cross fits

wear it

on the opposite side of the white stagecoach

on the opposite side of the white stagecoach
a man with a hostile bunch of green bananas
began to wail and scream like a sea anemone
deserted by the sea or an umbrella without rain.
he began throwing the bananas
at the women passengers who waved their ears
at him saucily and stifled their mirth.

in the morning he glares at me

in the morning he glares at me
and his yellow skin peels like fruit
and the sky comes into the room like butter
and his eyes are black as rainy stones
and the windows rattle with the air
and i shout
KEEP AWAY FROM MY SKIN!
MY HAIR'S COMING OFF!

the pain that i find in dust and disorder

the pain that i find
in dust and disorder
she carries on her back
like bread.

i asked for a ladder
for a gilded stagecoach
i asked for the moon

i found old tins in the cupboard
old tins, old dust
and her soft, soft skin.

fox colours of rust and brown
a nest of yellowed papers
and a bed full of books.

she gave me bunches
of words on a keyring
and question marks
to open locked doors.

the pain that i find
in dust and disorder
she carries on her back
like bread.

JOIE DE LIRE*

                                          we wander through Paris
                                          and our hair turns grey

inside the bookshop there's chaos;
a frenzy of mediations.
sentences from all over the world
leap from the shelves
green as sand, yellow as city streets,
dancing and arguing,
shouting slogans and reciting poetry
assaulting my brain cells
creating havoc in those tender circuits
of nerve and blood.

                    oh my head, imprisoned, exploding...
                    we're lost in this place
                    entangled in ourselves

                              the books
                              the pages
                              the hyphens
                              the full stops
                              the semi-colons

some unknown writer
beyond the publisher
            the printer
            the distributor
            the bookseller
with broken toenails and insomnia
some unknown author
writing beside a mountain
where the blood flows
in the shadow of green grain
in the shadow of a gun;

---

* *A big left-wing bookshop in Paris. (Now closed.)*

hundreds of thousands of unknown authors
chewing their cigars
picking their noses
excreting one word after the next

                my nerves
                stretched over bright mirrors
                jangle of cash registers
                jangle of skin and bone

our love turns in circles
we live in a web
our faces reflect
over and over

                in cafe mirrors
                shining teapots
                in steel and in china
                in brown and in green

beware of pickpockets
of thieves, invasions, revolutions
beware of changes in the colour of the sky
                        the skin
                        the breasts
                        the heartbeat

beware of your raw fingers, our indecision
of your clear sad eyes
                and my angry ones.

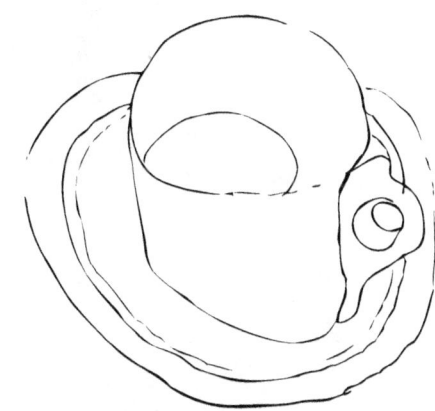

the weeds the witch and the roses

tonight
i shouted at you
i shouted at your back

you said nothing
i was behind you
behind you on the same bed

outside snow was falling

january.

twentyone years ago
we hid in the weeds
      under the witch
      among the roses

schoolgirls in blue and grey
there was you and me
the weeds the witch and the roses

the ghost
in our impossible machine
tracked us
twentyone winters,
the machine we invented
to fool the others

our secrets bound us
now they're out.

someone simple

one january
snow fell,
leeds wind.
i came back too early
and surprised you both.
you said you wanted
someone simple, like her
(not like me)
we walked
all three
in the grey snow

now it's night
the factory hums
a blue hyacinth is opening

in my white room.

absence

birdless days

the street wiped up like a frosty plate
windows rimed with cold white feathers

absence of leaves
absence of twilight

a cough echoes across puddles like iron

i wait for a letter like i wait for leaves

with hot house flowers

in my ungloved hands.

In the park gutted trees

In the park
gutted trees
watched me crawl
past the stone lion
and the four green swings
over the wet rot of winter
to your broken door.

You down there, in your bed down there

You down there, in your bed down there
and me up here, in my bed, writing.
You stretched out naked, saying
'Stay with me tonight' saying
'I'm so lonely' saying
'It hurts'.
And me climbing the stairs
my face in tatters
to my own bed.

THAT WORLD THROUGH THE WINDOW
IS A BAREFACED LIE

that world
through the window
is a barefaced lie.

there is ink on the yellow fields
and the moon
has been glued to the night
like an egg in a scrapbook.

bitter the battering moth
and the grasses that wind
shaken wave.

bitter the bird that flies
in ever smaller circles
as the poisoned world contracts.

there is a cold wind
inside me
and a bird
flies like a black rag
over the fields

behind my eyes.

A poem from Wales

O fire flames
oh orange peel night
oh whispering branches
oh burning pine
oh dust, dust, dust.
oh white hills
oh green sheep
oh slumbering lust
oh bowl of sky
oh history
oh scarlet hours
oh sharp axe
with fingernails of fire
oh wild clouds
with the shape of exploited beasts
oh time
stolen from us
with the black colours of mourning
oh time
lost with the emptiness of years
oh time
fashioned, claimed, regained
like mountains of gold.

oh time our time
evening time
with its still birds
morning time
with its slow opening eyes
yellow day time
blue nights under the wild moon
                    wild silver
                    wild goddess

TINA REID

Jill the Gripper

The outside night
Was Jack the Ripper's
East End street
Naughty Nineties,
Or a film of it
In black and white:

Slick wet paving,
Light in puddles
Growing lamp posts
Tall and straight
To poke their branches
Through the curtains
And crack the black
Inside night:

      'I can't
Tell need from greed'
She said.

Next time he entered her
He sank without trace, and
She licked the bed clean.

Morning on the Campsies

Here, the sky lies on the land all night,
Rolls over slow in the morning
And get up most reluctantly.

Colour sleeps somewhere else.
Those sheep you see are no-white,
Stones no-grey, grass no-green.

You couldn't have lost your blue glove here,
Though an hour or two
Will turn a glove blue

When the land comes out for the day
And it's the hills' turn to loll,
Round browned elbows,

Bent knees, bellies, oh you lovely!
To rub my face on.
Chance would be a fine thing.

Larks have it. To fly fell high,
To fall soft anywhere,
To touch just anywhere.

Shush lark
Watch out land!

Here comes a man
Well able to measure your length.

He will give you hair
It's hard to shake the sky out of.

The forester will throw over a dark cloth
To shut your noise a long night.

My boyfriend's Mum

My boyfriend's Mum's a man eater;
So is mine.

His once swallowed two whole,
One after the other.

They left her with chronic indigestion,
It was something cruel.

Her children still serve her remedies,
Wine or cigarettes or opportunities,

Each pill sugared
With a bit of themselves.

My Mum's more genteel.
She only had the one
And that she nibbled slowly.

Then started on the kids
And fell to with a vengeance.

Still, one day
These wicked old victims
Will die of malnutrition
And leave us in peace,
My boyfriend and me.

But oh the taste of people is sweet!

And I have a son
And he has a daughter
And we've always got each other.

Anniversary Invitation

You've had most things of mine,
Mined most things I had.

You've been in and looked them over,
Picked them up and weighed them up,
Pocketed some,
Put some down.

Anyway, since then
I've had the men in.

Had the lot taken.
Best way. It was already
Out of date or out of order,
It was all behind on the payments.

Now I keep an open house.
Empty, quiet. Like

A bowl in the hills
That fills with sun
And cloud and shadows of cloud
It never keeps.

You're welcome,

But you must come empty-handed

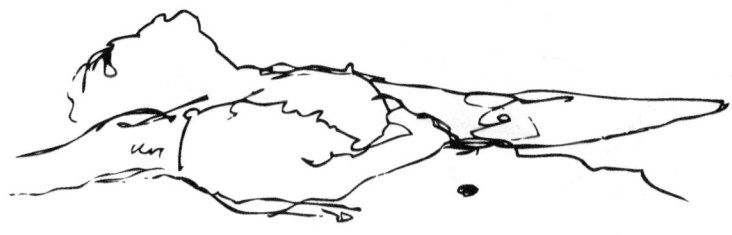

Ann's Poem

I won't have you take
my years from me.

They are jewels
I need not look at

(as pretty as
the bent shoes
of a woman
just died),

deposit account
I need not draw on,

on no account
of no account.

There, I need not look
before I lean or leap.

Take them, and I am
badly bruised. Senseless.

My heart is alive

My heart is alive

With maggots —
Sorry, feelings.
White, blind, timid.

Little larvae,

Will you live to fly?
To buzz and bother?
Be smashed, perhaps, off-hand?

Or will you always, tender,

Be stopped.
Smeared under a thumb
At birth.

Tower Hamlets Cemetery

Here the dead push up
Great fat hands of ivy,
Brambles strong enough
To garrotte the State, and
Thick-necked sycamores, better fed
Than the food that feeds them.

Here lie Flick, Flipping, Duck,
And Eliza Elizabeth Reason.
The salt of the earth
Returned to its proper place
In back-to-back, over-occupied
Tenement beds.

Such little beds. Either life
Cut the sleepers down to size
Or their legs are buried elsewhere.
Five to a grave sometimes they lie,
Most gone by their fifties
Against the national interest,

Tranquillised under five small stones:
Head, heart, crutch, knee and foot,
Where one large stone
Would have done for all
Had gratification been delayed
And paid for weekly through the Co-op.

Often they'll slump together
These stunted stones, cheek to shoulder,
Like sleeping children, or tumble
A sudden four foot down
When the multi-storied dead
Collapse like Ronan Point.

Shifty, that's the trouble
With cheap materials
And the cheap labour within.
So watch out, Fat-fingers:
The ground that keeps them down
May yet give under your feet.

The kestrel I saw circling
Was spotting live flesh.

See You

Your eyes are twin guns
Permanently cocked,
Multidirectional. Revolvers.

Little black mouths, silent
And bunkered. No way in.
The barrels behind are cold.

Their role is purely strategic.
They are ever on manoeuvres.
Shoot, why don't you.

Sleeper

Feather head,
Dead bird
In the crook
Of my collar bone.

Abandoned parcel
Containing everything.
It won't
Explode.

Arms legs
Left lying,
Shoe-laces,
Where they fell.

Back curved,
Curled shoot
Still stuck
In its old seed.

MICHELE ROBERTS

**'Women's entry into culture
is experienced as lack'**

he wishes he were a
one of those able to
dance and shake
breasts and belly and hips
loose, a
not-himself, nothing-but

he wishes they did not have a
hiding from it in his bed stillness
he bruises easily
they will suck the blood
from their own   afterwards
alone

he wishes he were still a little boy
so that he did not have to face them
telling him he is an oppressor
he needs them to scold him
darling oppressor

if he were a
he could join the   movement
but at least his   friends
are always   who struggle
he has nothing to do but
help them out of
silence he has
nothing else to do
with   oppression
nothing else
nothing

he wishes they had a   too
so they could all just be friends

Coniston New Year's Eve

in the light we climb
the mountain
called the Old Man
blue snow, dry, freezing, gives
our feet inch-holds
my boots dent his white head, I
grind rocks together, laughing

we sledge at midnight
eyes open upon the dark
only my sick stomach jumping
tells me one fall ends
another long
rush begins
I am a coward, fumbling
for your hand, a rosary
clenched, my muscles bang
the hurtling alleys of my fears
here I am
whooping into darkness, back
beyond, way beyond
puberty, blood out of the unnamed stone
plunging towards the woods, dark, and hairy
and the wet lake they fringe
its comfortable cavern, body-shaped

the sledge crashes
my cheek rips along
the water's rigid face
black ice scathes my spine
my eyes would poke the stars out
if they could

luminous, loading
more than half the sky
the Old Man floats
solidly
filling all that space of

loss, black loss, sweet black
with omni-
present white
I labour up the glassy slope
to start again
practising
letting go

mother, not letting you go
mother, letting you go

therapy 1

the site is old waste, raw
planks press the dust
metal bits tinkle and jam
weeds in a high tide
slap at a rubble beach

clear all this
build me a house, I want one
bright, cool as a palace
big as a funfair

hmmm? I propose
desperate, flirting

suddenly you say
you are no architect
you have no plans
there are no props

therapy 2

words, I whisper, I shout
are Trojan horses: the thief
in the night to the other asleep;
words are walls: I am besieged
and must defend

words, you say, are touch
are stepping-stones, images
exchange of gifts
words can be food

I'm all over the place
tough, sneaky, dogged
as Menelaus, Ulysses, Hector
and Paris, I'm
those chums in drag, a
pantomime beast with three legs
you are like Helen
only in this: your
beauty, your
patience, your other
loves besides me

co-operation, you say
no more plunder and pirating
inside my armour, I melt
as this, my long
my dangerous war ends
what I fear now is the plain
outside the city
love's wrestle
and peace

I have been wanting to mourn

I have been wanting
to mourn for a long time
to mourn for a past time
the bells of the ambulance this morning
beat at my head like angry fists
beat up my heart if I let them

in the French village of my childhood
each death, a steeple
rocked with our grief
so we assembled, we knew
who was meant, the bells told us
a clang for each year of the life
the black copes of the priests
blotted our bright tears
we sang rejoicing, God
had eaten another of us
we were still
his obedient children

years later in England
relatives began being
ticked off at Golders Green crematorium
meat out of the fridge
and into the fire
we prayed, our lips
stiff as the corpse
we were too young to see

and there have been friends
three of them
dead by suicide
I have hung their carcases in my throat

I want a funeral first
where I can mourn
mothering, and mourn
me, losing and lost, I

wanting her cradle
fat gobbler of gaps
and of anger, my consolation
the grave shovelled into my mouth

I have found women
to witness my loss
of blood of mother of childhood
called puberty (that is all
the word should be larger than that)
I call myself woman, I try to
it means accepting such pain:
no-one can ever love me
like that
nevermore
oh no never again

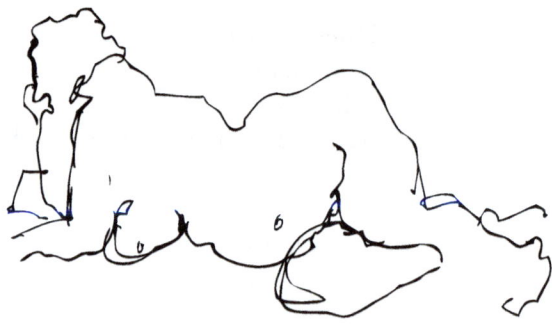

memories of trees

our confusion, to make men sound like gods:
unnatural woman, you are a tree
fixated, lost, with a deep gash
to be rained upon, rubbed up against
hidden in, struck down
sold, and burnt, your ashes
worthless

I plead, I can twist like metaphor
I approximate, I sway kneedeep
in ferns, I am cultivated, lovely
my bark is a thick plait
I rear myself near a woman lover
we are the hedges around farms
the milking-stool, the cradle
we furnish ships, and boxes
brooms, coffins, desks, and paper
we are your floors, your windows
our roots nourish us, twinned
labyrinthine memories, between us
passages, and gaps, and halts
the darkness wet beneath
the perplexed canopy of our hair

my father carves his name
on each in the plantation
clears our flowers, strips us
in a single word
I have stooped for years
I have smiled around him
now, when I fall upon him
crushing, still
he protests
you are my tree, only a tree

I too have words now, I have words
I am a woman in the city, I transform
nature, I survive

tempests; but my dreams
flower with him

the forest is long ago, is
deep coal
now
I pace the labyrinth
following the gold plait, thick, and knotted
when I find her, I am not only
heroine, but also
minotaur, she too

memories of trees
who never suffered pain
or yelled
or wept
or went away

Go away – for Pam

November Friday; two small
cars laden with five reach
the stone cottage empty
on weekdays, draining
the village of life —
our pleasure, our cash

I wish for constellations
certain in daylight, showing you
me, as we turn in a fixed
dance, towards and away
only distance speaking connection
far enough to see beauty (yours)
and to be blind to anger, tiredness, demands

you are my friend
I share a bed with you, cold
cracking air to splinters
we hug to survive

next day we climb seven hills
balancing bodies on
bony edge, the tender hollows
I hold in my hand
I suck horizons and taste
the rind of the sun, I blur
with the grey
orange and silver of trees

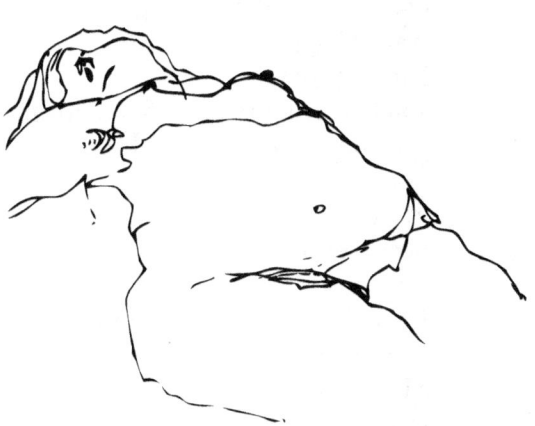

stiffened with frost, waving along
rigid in flurried motion, the twigs
fly up and back like quivering wires
woods indistinct, but every branch
rimed with clear shadow, and fields
wedges of green; firs
lift on my spine

turn my back, and the tree dance
carries on: impermanence, the exquisite game
every child plays
around the mother, now lost
now reappearing

while as for you?
I must shield, I must shield
myself.
I clasp the tops of hills, seven times
muscles and breath beating to
know for a second my place
between earth, air and peak
so as to shoot
down again, scramble and slide

over cards in the evening
you all happily row
I am afraid:
you like a mountain to fall in my mouth
your floods thick in my throat

you are my friend, I share a bed with you
over mountains I tell you my fears

I have let you in, I rush towards you
your hands my clitoris seed
a hill of sugar within me
pushing my throat
my lips to burst into
flower like fireworks
jolting neat patterns of stars
I am choking on sweetness and dark
I cry out to say so, I come
I praise you exceedingly
and you praise me, we
praise ourselves, look
at this rosy flush

sweeping through skies, it flings
redness on clouds, draws them, pushes them, soft
flesh aching to pleasure
the sun spills, we tremble, dissolve
we have flooded the sky with our redness, our wet
we rock on our lake, smiling and slippery, spent

the sky changes towards grey
sucking its light
back from the dark red of trees
soaking in colour, my hands on your hair
on your earth knowing russet, auburn, pale brown
and blood, we can let the sun
pale into sleep, tomorrow
another sunrise, sunset

punkrock; and Cocksparrow sings

I didn't expect it
(I like to know
what will happen, control it)
times have been hard, we were tired
(no you never get what you
want so don't
ask; if you are good, in fifty years' time
the revolution will give you
a book of instructions)

we went out dancing
in darkness, in glitter
an anniversary of sorts:
two women
six months of hard loving
hot little communion
with ninety others, your hands
root me, swaying in stars
your face, brighter than neon
I am sixteen as never then, fascinated
by sweat and satin and beer, the band
raucous, young boys on the dole
touching and innocent, yelling
mother, we are *so* bad, please
take us home
they hate the audience which
consumes them, their rage, their despair
I confront them, brazen
belonging: my hand in yours

back home to bed
you touched me gently: this could be
your benefit night
suddenly
you lay there laughing, your hand
leaping at me, come on
woman, come on; I flew

up and down
twice, and I came, it was simple
as that, I was amazed
and delighted, so proud
of myself, I didn't expect it
such prodigal
opening, such ease, and such
celebration

my bit of power
you never sang of, Cocksparrow
I compete with you still
last night I tried to forget
our separation, our
loneliness

I am abroad in a strange land

I am abroad
in a strange land
loving a man again

I thought: this
is the capable man, broad
bones and a frame for
lifting; he knows
words and
winds, combs seas, views far
where the marsh sags
where the stream gobbles
the forest's hem
he will join hands
to make me a path across

I thought: I'll be the gentle field
waving with grass and smells
where he lies down, I'll be
his summer, his
scarlet poppy drug to
soothe him, he will suck
my silk, my wiry stem

it grows dark
now: the winter afternoon
smears light with mud
the sea dashes against a fragile wall
the forest's gone, grey into grey
the marsh sedge waves and sighs
a single heavy mass
alive with goblins
shrieks of sudden pits
the track through fear
too narrow for my single eye to thread
he's gone, he's lost
and therefore I am also gone

he loses me, he flails
a broken windmill in the sky
he names
me as the storm, me
as the grabbing marsh;
I shake, I hide, I name
him as the hunter, he
shoots my violent woods
my knocking sea

when we search for one another
winds muffle our words
we must call
loud, and hard
our feet inch
the chaotic earth

the eldest son goes home

these are his bones
of his flesh
is this place made

the house grips him
with the teeth of love

silk beds are flung
for him, game slaughtered
at his mouth
whole generations
of feeding-bottles held

their gaze upon
the woman that he brings
is cold
her hands divide them
name her a whore, she goes
easily
naked and wet for him

his mother calmly dotes
on china figurines
his father bays and nags
to whack his penis off

while her man sleeps
the woman walks
she hangs alone upon a fence
watches the windy rooks
she tosses like a rag
on ploughed horizons
under lines of elms
barer than they
and very small
the house behind
belches, and smiles
and licks its maw

she feels alone so much
two nights of sleeplessness
can't shut her eyes
upon the homeward train
through the dark country
and the suburbs limps
her hero in his nasty dreams
he can't remember how
she fought for love of him
he carries cases up the chilly steps
she mocks her pretty skirt, she wants
to stick a hatpin in his eye

of her bones too
her flesh, and these two days
are children born

I have just come from the war

I have just come
from the war
I ducked about
like an ambassador
between contestants
with my pretty face
I jabbered on and on, I offered
anything for peace
lies kisses gold

it's an ill wind
that blows
nobody
any good change;
this wind blows on

I toss, fuss, protest;
I was a liar when I said
with clocks, maps, calendars
I was life's gaoler
now, there is only this wind

once I was a fat baby
once I was a star
once I was the teacher's darling
once the king chose me for his bride

now, far away
mothers wave farewell flags;
now, tiny
triangular jewelled jets
draw you through tropical nights

plants take their time
and seasons, and embryos
waiting for birth; I want to force
maytime, a bloodied spring
and your return

this wind blows on;
I am rebuilding my house
after the war
and with you gone

ANN OOSTHUIZEN

Bulletins from the front line

Regimental HQ, Ali's room;
Three windows, two desks, one bed
Papers everywhere.
Five women meet; a council of war
Our strategy still unspoken.
We are not in uniform, there are no medals,
We read the latest bulletins from the front line.
Carefully we study the terrain together.

Outside this blue room where dreams
Caress the tall green plants
Cars move on highways;
'Hey Baby', another woman raped.

We will assault all.
Tina, menacing at a window
Exquisite markswoman aims,
Her sniper's bullet finds unerring home.
Ali tunnels underground
Mining each foundation with precision
The city crumbles in surprise.
While Stef, laughing, flies overhead
Drops bombs without looking
Blows the world to smithereens.
What power, Sisters!
Michele's a pacifist, she says,
She disregards the war
Stands on the highest building
Look at me!
Her ear-rings challenge sun and moon,
Here it is, the war
In me, start here.

Five women plan in the smoke blue room;
Silence brings a pause for fear
Am I good enough? each one asks
Hesitating

The cold draught has caught
An old war-wound in me.
I smile, my death's-head smile
My skull cracks open.
I rattle goodbye across the railings.
As I pass through the park
There is no cover.
Shell-shocked, I limp home
my old bones aching.

I do not remember you with pleasure

I do not remember you with pleasure,
Sometimes when I sit, for example,
Next to a river shaded by tall trees
And hear the music of the water
As it shapes itself over the folded rocks,
I am reminded that we were once
Together by such a river
And that you held me there in your arms.
Then it is as if a deep shadow
Closes thick and dark over my mouth and nose.
My heart beats fast, in terror.
Is this what I felt then?

If we meet again in that other world
Two shades, as Milton said,
Insubstantial and without sex,
I will not run to you.
There is no part of me that consents
To being one with you.
You owned me once, and strutted over
The territory that was me,
Marking it with your mark, fencing it well,
Pulling out weeds that grew there.
You planted your seed in me,
You have fulfilled your god's command.
And I?
Barren is not sparse enough to describe
The fear and fright that grew in me
Only a tiny speck of mine remained.
You worked on that
And so did I; my guilt equal to your zeal,
But there was that in me which said:
I am not all yours.

Now you are dead.
I mourn for you.
I wish that you had known happiness
That you had found a gentle, wholesome love.
It was not so. My guilt made me spiky,
My barrenness grew sharp stones under your feet,
You did not find peace in your small-holding.

This plot of land is for sale no longer.
If we meet again, you will say:
What a rocky landscape, give me richer earth.
That is how I want it to be.
This land is mine.

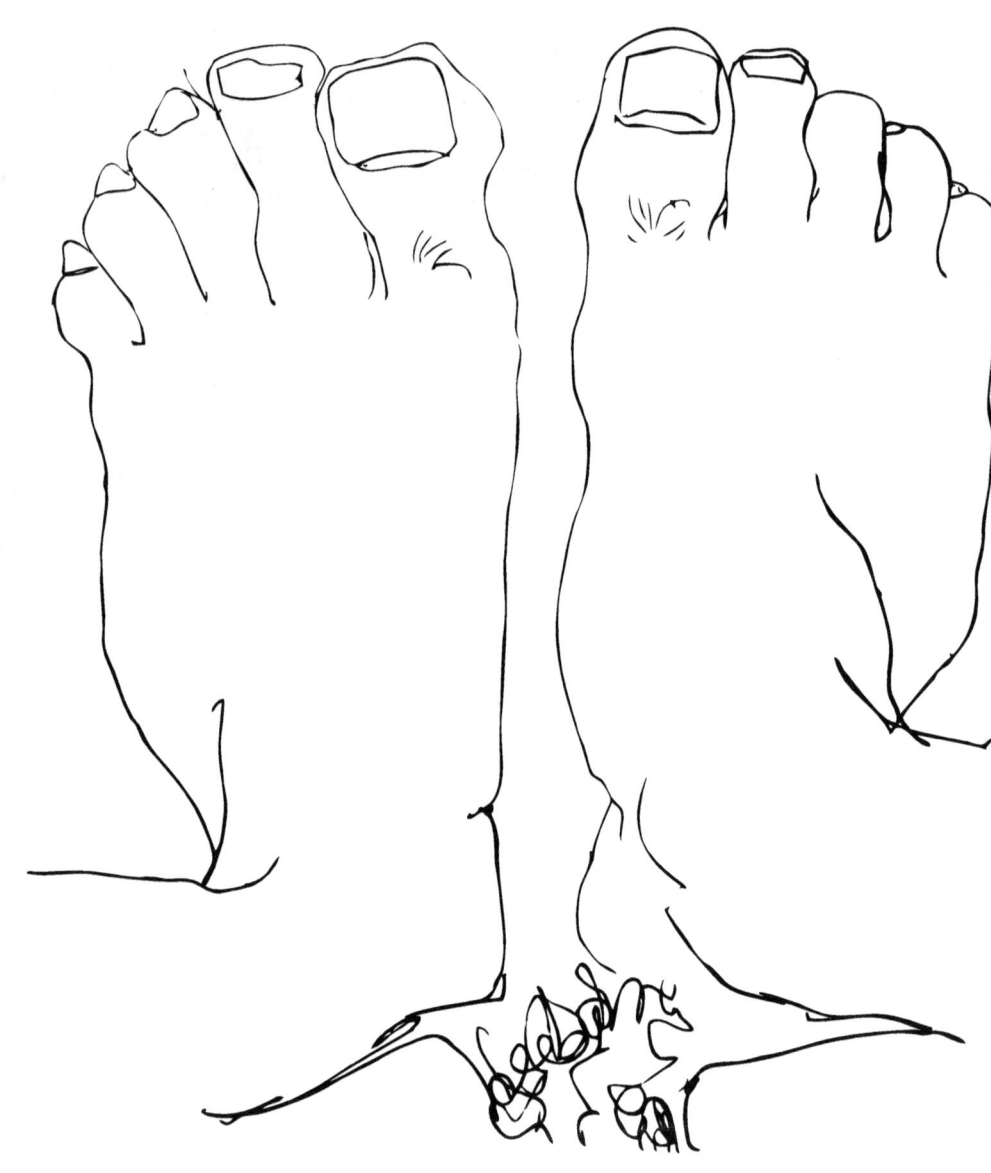

www.ingramcontent.com/pod-product-compliance
Lightning Source LLC
Chambersburg PA
CBHW071325040426
42444CB00009B/2084